An opinic

ART LONDON

Written by
Christina Rose Brown

Heather Phillipson, *THE END*, 2020. The Fourth Plinth (no. 13)

INFORMATION IS DEAD. LONG LIVE OPINION.

This book is useless. Everything you could want to know about art in London is online. Right?

Not quite. Because while you can find plenty of facts, opening times and history in the mess of information on Google, what's hard to find is vivid, concise opinion that will cut through the noise.

Art can be intimidating. Art can be mystifying. Art can be dull. There is a lot of it in London and not all of it is good. But there is great art: playful, uplifting, transformative. Let us show you where to see (and even buy or make) great art so that you can be inspired, challenged and dare we say it, even have fun.

Other opinionated guides:

East London
London Architecture
Vegan London
London Green Spaces
Independent London
London Pubs
Sweet London
Kids' London
Escape London
Eco London
Big Kids' London

Ugo Rondinone, *a sky . a sea . distant mountains . horses . spring .*, 2021. Sadie Coles HQ (no.52)

The Wallace Collection (no.58)

This page: Anne Norris, *Stack 9, Ultramarine Blue*, 2021. Frieze Sculpture Park
Opposite page: L. Cornelisson & Son (no.8)

da Vinci

WHAT'S SO GREAT ABOUT LONDON'S ART SCENE?

London's got it all. It's got more world-famous art museums, celebrated studios, high-end commercial galleries and avant-garde art schools than you can shake a paintbrush at. But, so what? Lots of cities around the world could say the same thing. New York hosts many of the most powerful (and wealthy) galleries, Miami's got ultra-luxe art fairs and Paris has the grand, historic Louvre, so what makes London so special?

It is London's subversive, rebellious streak that draws artists and art-lovers in like no other capital. Whether it's punks in the 70s, the wild irreverence of the YBAs, the birth of Pop Art in the 50s or the Pre-Raphaelites' orchestrating their radical shake-up of the art establishment in Victorian London, this city has always been one for challenging norms. All the best art pushes back at the status quo, forcing us to shake off our assumptions and see things anew – and that's why London is the best place in the world to discover art.

From the ever-controversial Fourth Plinth in Trafalgar Square (no.13), which showcases contemporary work on the grandest scale, to an outsider artist transforming discarded chewing gum into mini-masterpieces on the city streets (no.7), this counter-cultural dynamism still rules London's art scene today. It's home to some incredible galleries dedicated to amplifying marginalised voices, from Autograph (no.2) championing anti-racist photography to QUEERCIRCLE's (no.39) community-focused programme of LGBTQ+ artists.

One of the best things about London's art is how much of it you can see for free. Most major museums, including both Tates (no.35 and no.37) and The National Gallery (no.1) are proudly open to all, but what you might not know is that all the commercial galleries are also free to enter (even if the presence of security guards might suggest otherwise).

If you do want to start your own collection and support some emerging artists, you can peruse affordable and collectable artists' books at bookartbookshop (no.17) or find electrifying prints from up-and-comers at Jealous Gallery (no.5). And for those who'd rather make their own, we've selected the best art supply shops and classes so you can gather all the tools and knowledge you need for a major magnum opus.

When you know where to look, you'll see that art is seeped into every nook and cranny of this city. In fact, London has so much to offer it's easy to feel overwhelmed by the sheer number of temporary exhibitions and open studios there are to see, so let us guide you to the very best, the sometimes missed and the most inspiring art in London. Whether you're a gallery-hopper looking for something a little bit different, a wannabe collector, aspiring painter or just a little bit art-curious, this city has something for you. It's time to put on your shoes, dust off your oil paints and – with this book in hand – get ready to take on the (art) world.

Christina Rose Brown, 2022

Christina Rose Brown is a Brighton-born, London-based artist, educator and writer. She can normally be found in a gallery with her kids in tow.

BEST FOR...

Grand collections

Kenwood House (no.23) and The Wallace Collection (no.58) have lavish collections in stately-home settings. For a grand tour of Western art, head to the National Gallery (no.1). Alternatively, the perfectly preserved Sir John Soane's Museum (no.11) is as eccentric today as it was two hundred years ago.

Discovering new artists

You might not have heard of Guts Gallery (no.27), TJ Boulting (no.53) or The Approach (no.25) but these are the galleries to go to if you long to discover artists on the ascent. Regular group shows at the Sarabande Foundation (no.20) are a great way to see the next generation of pioneering creatives.

Affordable art

There are plenty of places to buy art in London that don't require a trust fund. Pick up reasonably priced prints at Jealous Gallery (no.5) and Print Club London (no.31), limited editions from established artists at Studio Voltaire (no.48) and one-of-a-kind artists' books from bookartbookshop (no.17).

Art trails

For a leisurely stroll with an artful twist, just follow The Line (no.30) – London's only permanent art trail. Short on time? Spot multi-coloured miniatures painted on discarded gum on the Millennium Bridge (no.7) or soak up street art in Shoreditch (no.33).

Classes and workshops

Ever visited a gallery and thought, 'I could do that'? Now's your chance. Take up film photography at Darkroom (no.21), perfect your portraits at The Royal Drawing School (no.3) or sharpen your pencils and try out a drop-in life drawing session at Candid Arts Trust (no.9).

Artistic gifts

Please your choosiest friends with some gorgeous stationery from Choosing Keeping (no.12). A voucher for M.Y.O's eclectic craft studio (no.43) is guaranteed to inspire, while a monograph from the carefully curated shelves at Hauser & Wirth (no.51) will be sure to impress.

Artful dining

For fine dining with a serious helping of fine art, make a reservation at sketch (no.57) – where opulent interiors come with a Michelin-starred menu – or drop by the ever-elegant Sessions Arts Club (no.4) for seasonal sharing plates surrounded by contemporary paintings.

Art supplies

If you want the best bargain brushes and acrylics then head to superstore Cass Art (no.18) or try L. Cornelissen & Son (no.8) for unusual heritage supplies. If you're looking for something hard-to-find, there's nowhere better than Atlantis Art Materials' (no.28) cavernous warehouse.

SEASONAL EVENTS

LONDON GALLERY WEEKEND

Every summer London's commercial galleries get together for a weekend of extended openings, art trails and special events, including artists' talks, drinks receptions and family-friendly workshops – the perfect excuse for a bit of gallery-hopping. A lot of amazing galleries and auctioneers close up shop over the weekend so this is your chance to take in some art – without having to take a day off.

Summer | londongalleryweekend.art

ART CAR BOOT FAIR

This isn't any old car boot sale. Instead of broken bric-à-brac, compilation CDs and bin bags stuffed with old clothes, you'll find uncover original artworks by contemporary artists – whether it's a one-off painting by a rising star or prints from Turner Prize winners. And while prices might be higher than your usual car boot, there are plenty of bargains to be found.

Spring | artcarbootfair.com

THE OTHER ART FAIR

Cut out the middleman at the annual London outpost of this global fair for independent artists. None of the exhibitors are represented by a gallery. Instead they are selected by a jury of art experts. With work starting at around £100 it's a dream destination for budding collectors.

Autumn | theotherartfair.com

PHOTO LONDON

Taking over Somerset House for a long weekend each May, this fair draws in top photography galleries from around the world. You're sure to find unmissable installations and exhibitions with a stellar roster of events alongside – we can't see any (ahem) negatives.

Spring | *photolondon.org*

INDEPENDENT CERAMICS MARKET

Pick up pots, vases and mugs directly from the artists. This market sets up its stalls every couple of months across a number of locations in London, but the best time to visit is definitely Christmas. It's the perfect place to buy gifts, or maybe just treat yourself.

Winter | *@independentceramicsmarket*

FRIEZE SCULPTURE PARK

The fair itself might be best left to industry insiders, but the outdoor sculpture trail is an absolute joy – it's fun, free and gives you the chance to get up-close to some blue-chip art in the glorious environs of Regent's Park.

Autumn | *frieze.com*

BOMB FACTORY OPEN STUDIOS

Once a year you can take a peek behind the curtain and visit these private artists' studios. It's not an exhibition (though there is plenty of work to view), but a chance to see the resident painters, sculptors and performance artists at work.

Spring | *bombfactory.org.uk*

1

THE NATIONAL GALLERY

Historic collection of Western art

Said to be one of the greatest collections of paintings in the world, and who are we to argue? With over 2,300 artworks on show, stretching out over eight hundred years, there's no chance that you'll ever feel like you've 'done' this goliath of great art. Choose from one of the mapped art routes to see a selection of key paintings (Stubb's surprisingly contemporary-feeling painting of a horse, *Whistlejacket,* is a must) or join a free tour of the collection highlights. Don't miss the recently acquired self-portrait by Renaissance trailblazer Artemisia Gentileschi – a true masterpiece and one of only about 20 works by female artists in the collection. Their big-ticket exhibitions are always among the best of the year, so don't miss out.

Trafalgar Square, WC2N 5DN
Nearest station: Charing Cross
Paid entry to some exhibitions
nationalgallery.org.uk

NATIONAL GALLERY
NATIONAL GALLERY

2

AUTOGRAPH

Photography centre championing diversity

Autograph is a gallery with a mission. Founded in the 1980s, it was the first space in the UK dedicated to showcasing diversity in the arts. Like a true superhero, it's still fighting for inclusion and social justice in the art world. Their programme amplifies marginalised voices and has included arresting works by Sunil Gupta as well as striking portraits by artist and activist Ingrid Pollard. They host monthly workshops for children with special educational needs and the building (designed by superstar architect Sir David Adjaye) is wheelchair accessible. They even use 100 percent green energy. Now that's a radically inclusive art gallery.

Rivington Place, EC2A 3BA
Nearest station: Shoreditch High Street
autograph.org.uk

ENTRANCE
ABDU'ALLAH

Zanele Muholi, *Somnyama Ngonyama, Hail the Dark Lioness*, 2017

3

THE ROYAL DRAWING SCHOOL

Old-school charm and new-school techniques

This place is serious about teaching drawing. Students at their intensive summer school have been known to shed tears over their charcoal sketches, but fear not, the teachers – who are all experts – give inspiring, if firm, advice so that even total beginners will be confident with a pencil before the week is up. Founded by King Charles III (and Catherine Goodman) only twenty years ago, the RDS has already taught a generation of emerging artists how to make their mark. The studio is pleasingly traditional with battered wooden easels and red velvet chaise-longues. Refresh yourself between sessions at nearby Origin, where students get a discount on steaming, small-batch coffee.

19–22 Charlotte Road, EC2A 3SG
Nearest station: Old Street
royaldrawingschool.org

5
44
40

4

SESSIONS ARTS CLUB

Heady clash of art and food

Exquisite dining meets fine art in this creative and culinary collaboration between painter-cum-entrepreneur Jonny Gent and celebrated chef Florence Knight. Enjoy seasonal small plates and signature cocktails in an old Regency courthouse, surrounded by a rotating collection of bold contemporary paintings and glamorously fading plaster walls. Although not technically a members' club, it is popular among the gallery glitterati and hard to get a table so make sure to reserve in advance. Then order a fresh raspberry bellini and the panisse (chickpea churros dipped in salt) and eavesdrop on the latest art-world gossip.

24 Clerkenwell Green ECIR ONA
Nearest station: Farringdon
sessionsartsclub.com

5

JEALOUS GALLERY

Art prints with attitude

Fancy yourself an art collector but don't quite have the resources to drop millions at an auction? Fear not. This Shoreditch gallery specialises in vivid prints from up-and-coming art stars as well as contemporary headliners like Camille Walala, the Chapman Brothers and David Shrigley. The staff are also all artists who make use of the in-house print studio and sell their work through the gallery. It's cool enough to impress even the most aloof critics but still totally affordable (prices start from around £30). Eat your heart out Charles Saatchi.

53 Curtain Road, EC2A 3PT
Nearest station: Shoreditch High Street
Other location: Crouch End
jealousgallery.com

JEALOUS
FINE ART PUBLISHING | SILKSCREEN & DIGITAL PRINT STUDIO | GALLERY SPACE

6

180 THE STRAND

A cavernous wonderland of digital art

This Brutalist office block turned gallery puts on ultra-immersive shows that are so ridiculously insta-friendly it would be easy to dismiss it all as style over substance. But what they might lack in subtlety they certainly make up for in fun. Get lost in the dark, labyrinthine basement and discover mind-bending installations hidden behind a maze of velvet curtains. This is a space that encourages pioneering artists to explore all the possibilities (and consequences) of AI and virtual reality with a regularly changing programme of ultra-immersive exhibitions – expect impressive tech and a full-on sensory overload.

180 The Strand, WC2R 1EA
Nearest station: Temple
Paid entry to some exhibitions
180thestrand.com

Caterina Barbieri, *Vigil*, 2022

7

CHEWING GUM PAINTINGS

Spat-out street art

Ever been out walking with your eyes on the ground and noticed a tiny splash of colour on the pavement? You might have stumbled across a mini-masterpiece. Better known as the Chewing Gum Man, artist Ben Wilson is brightening up London one piece of discarded gum at a time. His paintings are often dedicated to people who stop for a chat while he works, celebrating their friends or family or commemorating important events. Eagle-eyed pedestrians will spot his work all over the city but his most high-profile site is the Millennium Bridge, where right in the shadow of the Tate Modern, he has created his own open-air, public gallery. Outsider art in every sense.

Millennium Bridge, EC4V 3QH
Nearest station: Mansion House
benwilsonchewinggumman.com

17
09
2015

8

L. CORNELISSEN & SON

Beloved art supplies in a storied setting

Open the door to this much-loved fine artists' materials shop and you'll be transported back to the gas-lit streets of Victorian London. With original mahogany fittings and spindly shelves lined with old storage jars, it hasn't changed much since it first opened its doors in 1855 and began serving artistic luminaries like Walter Sickert. Colourful pigments are carefully weighed into large paper bags like flour, and they even have illustrated recipe cards so you can make your own watercolours. The staff (mostly young artists themselves) are both knowledgeable and encouraging. Try out their own-brand paints and discover new inspiring materials like metallic-hued oil bars or water-soluble charcoal.

105 Great Russell Street, WC1B 3RY
Nearest station: Tottenham Court Road
cornelissen.com

L. CORNELISSEN
PARIS VIENNA
Est. 1855

9

CANDID ARTS TRUST

Life drawing classes in a community hub

This do-it-all arts venue is a gallery space, creative studio, café and light-filled (albeit pleasingly scruffy) drawing lab. Drop-in life drawing (and maybe even life-changing) sessions happen several times a week (either evening, daytime or online), and basic materials are included in the very reasonable price. Sessions can be tutored or untutored, so whether you need guidance or just want to put on your headphones and get into the zone it's up to you. Come on Friday evenings for the more social Drink and Draw, where refreshments are available from a makeshift bar.

3 Torrens Street, ECIV INQ
Nearest station: Angel
candidartslondon.com

CANDID ARTS TRUST
Candid Courtyard
Cafe
Open
Candid Cafe

10

DOMOBAAL

Contemporary art hidden behind a historic façade

Behind the doors of this otherwise plain Georgian townhouse (and former lawyers' office) you may find some of the most optically exhilarating bursts of colour in the city. Entering an austere art gallery can feel intimidating but in this case, ringing the doorbell is strangely thrilling, as if you're about to cross the threshold into a whole new world. It might not be the most well-known gallery, but it is certainly influential. Shows change sporadically (so keep an eye on their dates) and lean towards site-specific installations which work with the building's original architecture, injecting a flash of lively creativity into this historic site.

3 John Street, WC1N 2ES
Nearest station: Russell Square
domobaal.com

Lothar Götz, *Salvation*, 2020

11

SIR JOHN SOANE'S MUSEUM

Utterly eccentric museum

The former residence of one of Britain's greatest architects (Soane designed the Bank of England and the Dulwich Picture Gallery [no.47]) still houses his vast collection of art and antiquities, arranged just as he left it – right down to the ancient sarcophagus in the basement. The tiny Picture Room is a marvel, full of hidden masterpieces such as Hogarth's *The Rake's Progress*, revealed at set intervals throughout the day from behind movable walls. There's a truly dizzying number of artefacts on display but if you find yourself wanting more, head to Pitzhanger Manor in Acton, Soane's country pile, which is now a contemporary gallery.

13 Lincoln's Inn Fields, WC2A 3BP

Nearest station: Holborn

soane.org

12

CHOOSING KEEPING

Heritage art materials from around the world

Possibly the most aesthetically pleasing stationery shop that has ever existed, Choosing Keeping specialises in the kind of high-quality papers, notebooks and artists materials that you'll be desperate to buy but won't dare to use. Tinged with a hefty dose of nostalgia for the stylish desktop accessories of a bygone era, everything here feels like an heirloom to be treasured. You can buy imported Japanese paints made to a hundred-year-old secret family recipe or gold-plated scissors forged in the Italian Alps. Never before have paper clips and rulers been so desirable.

21 Tower Street, WC2H 9NS
Nearest station: Covent Garden
choosingkeeping.com

13

THE FOURTH PLINTH

Subversive sculptures in the centre of London

The artworks selected to temporarily take up residence on Trafalgar Square's fourth plinth often make headlines – and not always for the right reasons. Before it raised art to great heights, the plinth was empty for over 150 years as funds ran out before the intended sculpture of William IV could be installed in the 1840s. With previous commissions including Katharina Fritsch's giant blue cockerel and Heather Phillipson's ice cream-eating drone, it's easy to see why they might have caused a bit of a stir. But we think that having such irreverent and insightful contemporary art in this prominent and historic location is a welcome change from the statues of old military men that are normally resident on such plinths – and it's always a great talking point.

Trafalgar Square, WC2N 5NJ
Nearest station: Charing Cross

Yinka Shonibare, *Nelson's Ship in a Bottle*, 2010

14

BARBICAN ART GALLERY

Iconic architecture, visionary art

This Brutalist masterpiece has a gallery space which is (unsurprisingly) all grey walls and concrete pillars. But (equally unsurprisingly) its exhibitions are just as idealistic and original as the Barbican itself. From Jean-Michel Basquiat to Lee Krasner and Carolee Schneemann, the gallery has hosted major retrospectives of some of the most interesting (and rebellious) artists of the 20th century. The curation is always exceptional, with plenty of archival material to explain historical and social contexts. Head downstairs to the Curve gallery for an experimental space that's seen everything from actual rain clouds to live birds playing electric guitars.

Silk Street, 2Y 8DS
Nearest station: Barbican
Paid entry to some exhibitions
barbican.org.uk

15

VICTORIA MIRO

Enduring art from a contemporary tastemaker

Victoria Miro is one of the ultimate grande dames of London's art scene. She opened her first space in 1985, trawling art-school degree shows to find talented graduates. There isn't a particular theme or medium that ties her artists together, but Miro has an eye for work that feels timeless and significant, like the vast rococo-style paintings of newcomer Flora Yukhnovich. Now, she represents international superstars like Grayson Perry, Idris Khan and Yayoi Kusama. The shows are reliably brilliant and always get people talking. Don't miss their hidden garden terrace – with its tree-lined pond and wooden benches, it's the perfect space for a moment of post-exhibition reflection.

6 Wharf Road, N1 7RW
Nearest station: Angel
victoria-miro.com

16

THE SHOWROOM

Non-profit gallery nurturing site-specific art

You can't miss this huge industrial space just off the Edgware Road. Depending on who's been commissioned to design their exterior mural, it could be bright yellow, purple and even checked. But, of course, the art isn't only on the outside. With a programme of just four exhibitions a year, emerging artists (particularly those who haven't yet been exhibited in the capital) are given the time to take risks, experiment and create site-specific works. And they certainly know how to pick them – previous alumni include Sam Taylor-Johnson, Mona Hatoum and Eva Rothschild.

63 Penfold Street, NW8 8PG
Nearest station: Edgware Road
theshowroom.org

BOSCOBEL
STREET NW8

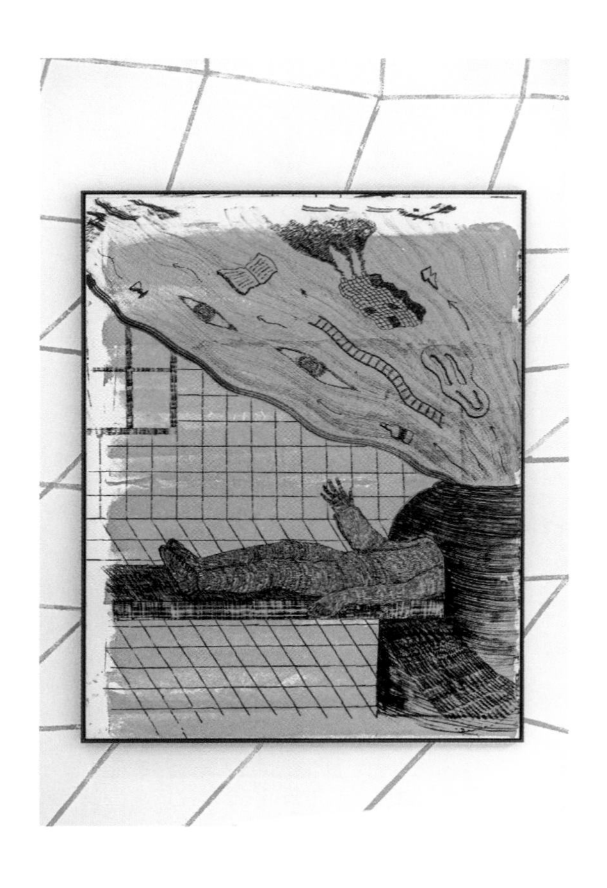

This page: Adam Shield, *Scanner (II)*, 2022

Opposite page: Adam Shield, *Control*, 2022

17

BOOKARTBOOKSHOP

Emporium of uniquely wonderful books

A perfectly bound storybook for spiders, written in spider language and designed to be hung in a spiral from the ceiling? An exquisite pop-up book made from paper-thin preserved apple slices? Whatever kind of art books you're searching for, this tiny bookshop has floor-to-ceiling shelves teetering with handmade and limited edition artists' books. Rifle through stacked-up boxes to uncover the weirdest (and most marvellous) reads of your life – you won't find these on Amazon, this is a physical store in its prime.

17 Pitfield Street, N1 6HB
Nearest station: Old Street
bookartbookshop.com

Charles
Square
Pitfield
Street
bookartbookshop
bookartbookshop

18

CASS ART

Art megastore

With its brightly lit, shiny shelves and endless special offers, Cass Art has the vibe of a very arty supermarket. The flagship in Angel is art-geek heaven, with three floors filled with brushes in every possible size and paint sets to suit any budget (their own brand range is brilliant and affordable). Even if you don't know your HB pencil from a blending stick, the staff (most of whom are artists) regularly run demonstration tables where you can try out products as well as hosting regular artist-led workshops. Their end of season sales are a regular pilgrimage for budget-conscious art students and perfect for a trolly dash.

66–67 Colebrooke Row, N1 8AB
Nearest station: Angel
Other locations: multiple, see website
cassart.co.uk

CASS ART LONDON
COLEBROOKE ROW
WATER
PAPER

19

CAMDEN ART CENTRE

Ultramodern art in a timeless setting

What is it that makes this north London institution so brilliant? Is it the beautiful Victorian architecture? The light-filled gallery spaces? The frankly fabulous café with its Italian-inspired menu and secluded garden? Maybe it's all of the above, alongside a programme that includes some of the most trail-blazing contemporary artists working today, often creating site-specific installations that always surprise. Regular events such as curator-led tours and art courses for kids (whose work is then displayed alongside the artists) ensure everyone can get involved. Oh, and don't forget to check out the small (but very well-stocked) bookshop.

Arkwright Road, NW3 6DG
Nearest station: Finchley Road and Frognal
Paid entry to some exhibitions
camdenartcentre.org

Allison Katz, *Artery*, 2022

20

SARABANDE FOUNDATION

Fearless creative community

When Lee 'Alexander' McQueen passed away in 2010 he didn't just leave behind an era-defining fashion portfolio, but also a boundary pushing foundation for young creatives. Artists selected for the programme reflect McQueen's ground-breaking spirit and several, including Rosie Gibbens (known for her absurdist soft sculptures, *pictured*), are already making waves. The converted stables are predominantly used as private studios, but there are regular group shows by the resident artists so keep an eye on their website for details.

22 Hertford Road, N1 5SH
Nearest station: Haggerston
Other locations: Tottenham
sarabandefoundation.org

Sarabande Summer Show, 2022

21

DARKROOM

Sanctuary for analogue enthusiasts

Does the metallic aroma of developer and fixer bring you out in nostalgic goosebumps? Whether you're a seasoned photographer or don't know your aperture from an enlarger, you can indulge all your analogue urges at Darkroom. Sign up as a member to make use of their processing facilities or take a class to discover every aspect of film photography, from the chemical magic of solarisation to printing your own photos. Housed in an underground car park on a residential estate in Camden, it's not the most salubrious location but you'll forget the outside world once you're basking in the scarlet glow of the safety light.

71 Marsden Street, NW5 3JA
Nearest station: Kentish Town West
darkroomlondon.org

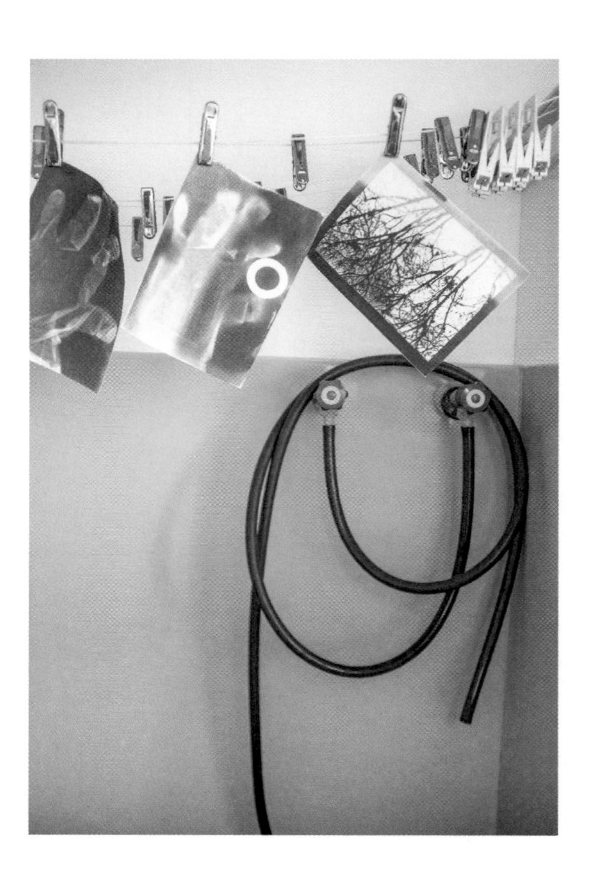

FC
GLAZING
MACHINE
NEGATIVE

22

OOF GALLERY

Ballsy art gallery next to the Spurs' stadium

Fine art and football might seem unlikely bedfellows, but at OOF they come together like Posh and Becks. It's the world's only contemporary arts space dedicated to the beautiful game and its team sheet includes some of the UK's most established artists alongside rising stars. Located in a stunning Georgian townhouse, it sits next to White Hart Lane and once housed the Spurs Supporters' Club in the 1980s. The building was recently renovated and enveloped into the grounds of the newly built stadium. Enter through the gift shop.

744 High Road, N17 0AP
Nearest station: White Hart Lane
oofgallery.com

BALLS, 2021

TOTTENHAM

AIA

23

KENWOOD HOUSE

Neoclassical mansion bursting with art

This 18th-century villa on the edge of the incomparably magnificent Hampstead Heath is home to one of the largest art collections ever bequeathed to the British public. It's free to visit and full of flamboyant interiors and luminous masterpieces, including one of Rembrandt's searing self-portraits and a tempestuous view of the Heath by Constable (find it in Lady Mansfield's Dressing Room). The parkland surrounding Kenwood House hosts sculptures by Henry Moore and Barbara Hepworth so make sure to find them before you set off for a dip in one of Hampstead's famous ponds.

Hampstead Lane, NW3 7JR
Nearest station: Hampstead Heath
english-heritage.org.uk

24

WHITECHAPEL GALLERY

Legendary east London gallery

The Whitechapel is a bit like that friend you can always trust to recommend great bands before they get famous – Jackson Pollock, Mark Rothko and Frida Kahlo all had their first UK shows here. While the original building might seem traditional from the outside (that said, look closer and you'll see a flurry of shimmering foliage by artist Rachel Whiteread embedded in the façade), they continue to be forward-thinking with the artists they show. Their triennial London Open exhibition has launched many famous names (Paula Rego, Grayson Perry and Anish Kapoor are all alumni) so it's worth putting in your calendar.

7–82 Whitechapel High Street, E1 7QX
Nearest station: Aldgate East
Paid entry to some exhibitions
whitechapelgallery.org

THE PASSMORE EDWARDS LIBRARY
HITECHAPEL ART GALLERY
UNDERGROUND
ALDGATE EAST STATION
Whitechapel Gallery

25

THE APPROACH

Contemporary art above a pub

Come for the eye-opening contemporary art, then stay for a pint and some triple-cooked chips. While some boozers have a function room upstairs, The Approach Tavern has a world-class gallery. The mission of the gallery is to showcase work by London-based artists at the beginning of their careers and many of their original roster have already gone on to international success. Just off Victoria Park, the surrounding area is full of galleries (Auto-Italia, Cell Project Space and Maureen Paley) all within walking distance, so use the pub as a base for a gallery crawl.

47 Approach Road, E2 9LY
Nearest station: Bethnal Green
theapproach.co.uk

THE APPROACH TAVERN
FREE
The approach

This page: Kira Freije, *meteorites*, 2022

Opposite page: Sara Cwynar, *Marilyn*, 2020

26

CHISENHALE GALLERY

Charity-led space for artistic innovation

Housed in an old brewery on a residential street in Hackney, Chisenhale was founded as a non-profit by a group of artists with a taste for the unconventional. Today it retains its reputation for supporting emerging practitioners to produce groundbreaking work – rather than just exhibiting them. Artists are invited onto a two-year program where their ideas are developed into seriously ambitious large-scale projects. Check their listings as each exhibition also comes with a programme of on- and off-site events, with everything from curators' tours to artists' talks and wonderfully messy kids' workshops.

64 Chisenhale Road, E3 5QZ
Nearest station: Bethnal Green
chisenhale.org.uk

Rachel Jones, *say cheeeeese*, 2022

27

GUTS GALLERY

New kids shaking up the art world

In 2019, founder and director Ellie Pennick basically ripped up the rule book on how galleries should work with artists. At this radical newcomer they don't represent artists, they 'champion' them, offering support and mentoring alongside exhibitions while also providing fair pay to everyone they work with. Expect bombastic but thought-provoking paintings from recent graduates of the Royal College of Art. If you really fall in love with one of the works on display, the gallery provides installment-based payment plans designed to make art collecting more accessible. What started as a nomadic pop-up now has a shiny new permanent home in Hackney. Is this the future of galleries? We hope so.

Unit 2 Sidings House, 10 Andre Street, E8 2AA

Nearest station: Hackney Downs

gutsgallery.co.uk

Sophie Vallance Cantor, *AUTISTIC BITCH*, 2022

28

ATLANTIS ART MATERIALS

Scruffy but wonderful art supplies warehouse

If there are any art materials that Atlantis doesn't stock, they probably aren't worth having. Totally independent and founded by artists in the 1970s, it now proudly claims to be the biggest art shop in the UK. Housed in an unassuming warehouse in an industrial corner of London Fields, it has the feel of a wholesale depot and stocks every type of paint, printmaking ink and canvas you could imagine. Air-drying clay? Gold leaf? Kids' art smocks? Tick. Tick. Tick! So whether you're a seasoned artist or a total beginner, enjoy a leisurely browse, watched over by resident shop cat Kiki who sleeps on a comfy bed of recycled packaging materials and acid-free tissue. But be careful, she bites!

Unit 1 Industrial Centre, Bayford Street, E8 3SE

Nearest station: London Fields

atlantisart.co.uk

29

THE LORD NAPIER STAR

London's most decorated pub

A pub that is literally a work of art, the Lord Napier started its life back in the 1860s as an East End alehouse serving local factory workers. When its doors closed in the 90s, graffiti artists turned the pub into a colourful, collaborative canvas. Recently redeveloped, it now serves craft beers and Thai-inspired burgers to a new generation of Hackney residents. Fortunately, it not only still retains its distinctive street-art façade but also local artists are occasionally invited to add to its murals, ensuring it continues to represent the area's heritage. Grab a seat on the roof terrace for a view of Anish Kapoor's divisive *Orbit* sculpture in the Olympic Park.

25 White Post Lane, E9 5EN
Nearest station: Hackney Wick
lordnapierstar.co.uk

OZONE
THE LORD NAPIER

30

THE LINE

London's first dedicated public art trail

Wander along the East End's scenic waterways, all the way from the Olympic Park to Greenwich Peninsula, and discover monumental installations hidden among canals and industrial sites. The signage is few and far between, but maybe that just adds to the treasure hunt authenticity of this urban art trail. You'll come across Rana Begum's ethereal floating mesh sculptures and several innovative iterations of local legend Madge Gill's paintings (including one covering the side of a bridge over the River Lea) along the way. It should take about three hours to complete – if you don't take a wrong turn.

Queen Elizabeth Park, E20 2A
Nearest station: Stratford
the-line.org

Rana Begum, *Catching Colour*, 2022

31

PRINT CLUB LONDON

Lively studio for print pros and beginners

Ever visited a gallery and thought: 'I could do that?' Well, Print Club London exists to make that idle dream a reality. With their screen-printing sessions for beginners covering all the basics in a single day, you'll be giving Andy Warhol a run for his money quicker than he could say Campbell's Soup Cans. And you'll be in good company – their open-access print studio counts many successful printmakers as regulars. Not feeling creative? Look at their online gallery and shop for surprisingly affordable handmade prints made by studio members.

10–28 Millers Avenue, E8 2DS
Nearest station: Dalston Kingsland
printclublondon.com

PRINT
CLUB
LONDON

32

CARIBBEAN FRUIT

Street sculpture celebrating immigration and diversity

Home-cooked food, family gatherings and the Caribbean islands – Veronica Ryan's marble and bronze fruits speak directly to east London's diasporic communities, honouring the Windrush generation and their legacy. Placed on a street corner near Hackney Central, you are likely to see passers-by perched against them, or overhear conversations about old family recipes for Jamaican breadfruit rundown and the best way to eat a custard apple. This is public art done right: beautiful, meaningful and accessible to all.

The Narrow Way, Mare Street, E8 1HL
Nearest station: Hackney Central

Veronica Ryan OBE, *Custard Apple, Breadfruit and Soursop*, 2021

33

ALTERNATIVE LONDON STREET ART TOUR

The original (and best) East End art tour

Know London like the back of your hand? Just visiting on a daytrip? This two-hour guided stroll round the open-air gallery that is the East End will teach you something new every time. From early Banksys to ceramic Invaders, explore this creative corner of London, revel in the transient nature of urban art and learn the stories behind the murals and street sculptures, including fishermen on the roof of the Truman Brewery and miniature bronze works by Jonesy hidden on top of streetlights.

19 Hessel Street, E1 2LR

Nearest station: Aldgate East

alternativeldn.co.uk

Mark Jenkins, *Fisherman*, 2018

34

TURNING EARTH

Meditative ceramics studio for all

There is nothing so grounding as rolling and shaping a clod of clay, or so magical as the alchemy of wet earth transforming into pottery. Even if you are beneath a commuter train line. In fact, that's the point. The folks at Turning Earth know that time spent working with your hands is the perfect antidote to hectic city life. Classes can be booked in blocks of 8 or 12 lessons and their expert teachers can guide you through everything from the basics of pinch pots to throwing elaborate vases. Experienced ceramicists can also become studio members (be warned, their Hoxton studio has a long waiting list). You'll find this airy, industrial space is the perfect place to escape from the hustle and bustle, even as the commuter train rumbles overhead.

Arch 403, Cremer Street, E2 8HD
Nearest station: Hoxton
Multiple locations, see website
turningearth.org

35

TATE BRITAIN

The UK's premier art establishment

While it might seem like the sensible older sibling to the younger and hipper Tate Modern, the former National Gallery of British Art is anything but fusty. Yes, there are plenty of pastoral Constables in the collection, but temporary exhibitions and regular commissions from contemporary artists ensure it stays fresh. The main collection is a chronological best of British, stretching back 500 years. Skip past the bucolic landscapes and head to the Pre-Raphaelite room for some OTT Romanticism, or the 1960s to witness a technicolour explosion of Pop Art. Afterwards head to the café where you can have a cuppa beneath a captivating mural on motherhood by up-and-coming British artist France-Lise McGurn.

Millbank, SW1P 4RG
Nearest station: Pimlico
Paid entry to some exhibitions
tate.org.uk

TATE

Cornelia Parker, *Cold Dark Matter: An Exploded View* (1991), 2022

36

THE PAINTED HALL

Baroque painting on the grandest scale

The opulent dining hall of the Old Royal Naval College, strikingly situated on the banks of the Thames, takes the art of the mural to the utmost extreme. Kings and queens gambol with Greek gods and mythical beasts in this immersive artwork designed by 18th-century artist Sir James Thornhill. Often called London's Sistine Chapel, it is breathtaking and considerably less busy than its Italian counterpart. Reopened in 2019 after undergoing a major two-year restoration project, every inch is painted with *trompe-l'œil* effects, right down to the 'carved' details on the columns. Tours are included in the entry fee and little art-enthusiasts can pick up free explorer's bags full of toys and games that will bring the epic masterpiece to life.

King William Walk, SE10 9NN

Nearest station: Maze Hill

Paid entry

ornc.org

37

TATE MODERN

Temple to modern art

If art was a religion then, without doubt, Tate Modern would be the cathedral. It's a true behemoth of a museum with a collection that spans all that is great and good from 20th- and 21st-century art. The main gallery is free to visit and arranged thematically. It's already more than you'd be able to see in one trip, and regular (paid) exhibitions and special events mean that there is always something new to discover. Given that it regularly tops the list of most visited UK attractions, we're probably already preaching to the converted.

Bankside, SE1 9TG

Nearest station: Blackfriars, Southwark

Paid entry to some exhibitions

tate.org.uk

38

WHITE CUBE

Homegrown contemporary art powerhouse

Back in the 90s White Cube's founder, Jay Jopling, built his name managing up-and-coming artists like Damien Hirst and Tracey Emin, courting the tabloid press and generally shaking up the art world. His flagship space, a converted warehouse in Bermondsey, is the biggest commercial gallery in Europe and has a roll call of artists to rival a major museum with Julie Mehretu, Anthony Gormley and Anslem Kiefer all featuring. From there, it's also worth exploring Jopling's nearby Bermondsey Project Space to discover the art stars of tomorrow.

144–152 Bermondsey Street, SE1 3TQ
Nearest station: London Bridge
whitecube.com

Louise Giovanelli, *Prairie*, 2022

39

QUEERCIRCLE

Creative centre for the queer community

For years we've watched LGBTQ+ spaces close one by one, but now, thank goodness, there's a glorious new wave of venues dedicated to amplifying queer voices. QUEERCIRCLE launched its multi-use arts space with a host of iconic artists, critics and campaigners on its board of directors. The gallery also has a library and workshop room where you can find drawing sessions for LGBTQ+ families and adult art classes. The inaugural exhibition saw artist Michaela Yearwood-Dan install a curved bench painted with a floral mural where visitors can sit and reflect, surrounded by joyous colour. It is an artwork created to feel like both a sanctuary and a community hub – which is, coincidentally, a perfect description of this new gallery.

3 Barton Yard, SE10 0BN
Nearest station: North Greenwich
queercircle.org

ON
RED
HILL
Me and White Supremacy
CHAVS
THEPHOTOBOOK
CLAUDE CAHUN

Happy Families
Olivia
Laing
Funny Weather
How
Be
An
Artist

40

ART SOCIAL CLUB

Paint your own masterpiece in one evening

You *could* spend years at art school studying golden ratios and colour theory – or you could save yourself a lot of time (and money) and create a wall-worthy artwork in just one class. Choose from a selection of templates that you can stencil straight onto the canvas, grab your paints and start colouring it in (from abstract nudes to van Gogh's blossoming branches, all you need to do is stay within the lines to make an expert artwork). Sit down at a table easel underneath twinkling fairy lights strung from the rafters of this welcoming studio and enjoy the gentle ambience. The process is broken down into steps so simple that even the most unconfident artists will leave feeling like Michelangelo.

34 Tooley Street, SE1 2TU
Nearest station: London Bridge
artsocialclub.co.uk

41

BOLD TENDENCIES

Car park + pink staircase + bar = art space

In the mid-2000s Peckham was the place to be for the art crowd. While most art school graduates have since been priced out, their legacy remains with the achingly hip Bold Tendencies. Once a car park, it's now part rooftop bar, part public art space and 100 percent Instagrammable thanks to the panoramic city views and bubblegum pink staircase (which is also an art installation). Open between May and September each year, they commission site-specific artworks with a focus on the genuinely fun and interactive. Past works have included an Afrofuturist slide, a mechanical bull you can actually have a go on and a room filled with hundreds of colourful balloons.

Floors 7–10, Multi-Storey Car Park,
95a Rye Lane, SE15 4ST
Nearest station: Peckham Rye
boldtendencies.com

Simon Whybray, *hi boo i love you.*, 2016

Harold Offeh, *Hail the New Prophets*, 2021

42

NOW GALLERY

Shape-shifting exhibition space

The glass building that Now Gallery inhabits (in the increasingly artful Greenwich Design District) looks like it should be a fancy office block, not a platform for art, fashion and design. It may not be the most atmospheric gallery, but with its panoramic windows and open-plan space, it does lend itself to the large-scale immersive installations that have become their raison d'être. Past exhibitions have seen it transformed into a dreamlike jazz club and an overgrown arboreal maze. The young artists that they work with think big – creating ambitious work that is always daring and bold. Combine it with a visit to nearby QUEERCIRCLE (no.39).

Peninsula Square, SE10 0SQ
Nearest station: North Greenwich
nowgallery.co.uk

Lydia Chan, *Your Ship Has Landed*, 2022

43

M.Y.O

Evening classes for the art-curious

Got a hankering for some arts and crafts but not quite sure where your talents lie? There are plenty of classes at 'Make Your Own' to get you started, from lino-print tea towels to embroidered wall hangings and their signature ceramic boob pots. The cosy Bermondsey studio has the best stocked cupboard we've ever seen: jars of beads, spools of ribbons in rainbow hues and patterned fabric off-cuts abound. Classes are short but sweet (only lasting a couple of hours) – just perfect for dipping your toe in (some paint).

82 Redcross Way, SE1 1HA
Nearest station: Borough
myo.place

44

LEAKE STREET TUNNEL

Make your mark on London's longest graffiti wall

At this constantly evolving street art site beneath Waterloo station, graffiti is not just tolerated – it's actively encouraged. The walls are repainted regularly so there'll be something different to see each time you visit, whether it's an elaborate mural by a well-known artist or a hodgepodge of tags by local kids. Everyone can get involved, so pack a spray can if you fancy yourself as the next Banksy. Or, if you're in a more contemplative mood, sit back at one of the tables from the independent bars situated within the tunnel and watch the artists at work.

Leake Street, SE1 7NN
Nearest station: Waterloo
leakestreetarches.london

DON'T
BELIEVE

45

HAYWARD GALLERY

Temporary exhibitions challenging the status-quo

It might be smaller than the neighbouring Tate Modern, but the Hayward certainly packs a punch. While it doesn't have its own permanent collection, the gallery does host a series of zeitgeist-capturing group shows and career-defining retrospectives for the likes of Louise Bourgeois and Bridget Riley. Housed in the Southbank Centre, many artists have incorporated the iconic building into their work, whether it's Carsten Höller's slides or Antony Gormley's cast-iron figures perched on the roof. Finish your trip with a stroll along the Thames and browse second-hand art books at the Southbank Book Market underneath Waterloo bridge.

Belvedere Road, SE1 8XX

Nearest station: Waterloo

Paid entry to some exhibitions

southbankcentre.co.uk

Lina Iris Viktor, *Eleventh*, 2018

HAYWARD GALLER

HAYWARD GALLERY
Gursky

46

THE ICA

Iconic anti-establishment institution

It might be housed in the sovereign's own Crown Estate, but this gallery is anything but traditional. In fact, the Institute of Contemporary Arts has championed radical culture ever since its foundation in 1946. Conceived as a place where artists could be free from the conservative constraints of the Royal Academy, that non-conformist spirit lives on in its progressive programming of exhibitions, art-house films and live performances. Take a piece of the avant-garde home with you by picking up an independently published artist zine from the much-loved bookshop. Exhibitions are regularly open until 9pm and the cinema and bookshop close even later, so perfect for an artistic evening after work.

The Mall, SW1Y 5AH

Nearest station: Charing Cross

Paid entry to some exhibitions

ica.art

Institute of
Contemporary
Arts

47

DULWICH PICTURE GALLERY

The oldest public art gallery in London

Built by Sir John Soane in 1817, this south London favourite is home to a stellar collection of old masters. The raised skylights (an innovative design that has since become standard for grand galleries around the world) flood the space with perfectly diffused light ensuring the pigments look as luminous now as they did when they were first painted. Temporary exhibitions often introduce lesser-known historical artists or contextualise more modern works alongside their classical collection. Take a detour to the café to indulge in delectable all-day brunch dishes while looking out over three acres of elegantly landscaped gardens.

Gallery Road, SE21 7AD
Nearest station: West Dulwich
Paid entry to some exhibitions
dulwichpicturegallery.org.uk

48

STUDIO VOLTAIRE

Radical gallery for underrepresented artists

London is full of impressive galleries, but this non-profit art centre might just be the most innovative of them all. With a verdant permanent installation (and kitchen garden) by Anthea Hamilton right at the entrance, you're part of an artwork before you've even stepped through the door. Studio Voltaire puts on pioneering exhibitions by risk-taking artists (often their first solo shows in the UK) in a recently renovated Methodist church, expanded to create studio space for 75 artists. They also have one of the best selections of limited edition artworks available. Shop for signed and numbered prints and brilliantly bizarre objects (like hand-painted washing-up gloves) before grabbing a table at their on-site café for a home-brewed kombucha and a delicious lunch sourced from Hamilton's garden.

1A Nelsons Row, SW4 7JR
Nearest station: Clapham Common
studiovoltaire.org

William Scott, 2021

49

SOUTH LONDON GALLERY

Socially-conscious gallery south of the river

The jewel in the crown of the south London art scene is, without a doubt, this majestic gallery. Now split between two sites (including the recently converted Fire Station, *pictured*), it was originally established in the 19th century to promote culture and education in the area. Since then, its reputation for doing exactly that has only flourished. Recent exhibitions have been typically avant-garde, such as Ann Veronica Janssens' rideable bikes and Shamica Ruddock's cosmic soundscapes. Don't miss the garden designed by Mexican artist Gabriel Orozco (open weekends only) – a tranquil spot that feels a million miles from Peckham Road.

65 Peckham Road, SE5 8UH
Nearest station: Peckham Rye
southlondongallery.org

ENGINES

50

GAGOSIAN

International powerhouse with big-ticket artists

Larry Gagosian is thought to be the world's richest art dealer, and everything about the Mayfair branch of his gallery empire screams money – from the imposing purpose-built space to the besuited security guards and the big-ticket artists on show (Damien Hirst and the estate of Picasso are both on Larry's books). While it all seems designed to intimidate, if you make it through the door they are very friendly. Exhibitions are always free and you are pretty much guaranteed to see something astonishing.

20 Grosvenor Hill, W1K 3QD
Nearest station: Bond Street
Other locations: Mayfair, King's Cross
gagosian.com

51

HAUSER & WIRTH

Spectacular art in the heart of Mayfair

Not only is it one of the most prestigious galleries in the world, but Hauser & Wirth actually has a real-life Princess working with them (Eugenie York is a director). It also represents some serious art-world royalty like Cindy Sherman, Jenny Holzer and Frank Bowling. It currently occupies two sites on Saville Row – the North Gallery with its enormous floor-to-ceiling windows is perfect for impressive paintings and large-scale installations, while the South Gallery houses a bookshop (where you can find a selection of their own excellent publications, as well as catalogues and artists' books) and a more intimate exhibition space.

23 Saville Row, W1S 2ET
Nearest station: Oxford Circus
hauserwirth.com

HAUSER & WIRTH

Luchita Hurtado
I Live
I Die
I Will Be
Reborn
Publication
Marcel Duchamp
DELL

Painting
Rashid Johnson
Rashid Johnson
Rashid Johnson
THE TWIN PAINTINGS
Ursula
Ursula
In the Black Fantastic
Ekow Eshun
Hurtado
Luchita Hurtado
Luchita Hurtado
Luchita Hurtado

52

SADIE COLES HQ

Cool art with a warm welcome

A trendsetting gallery in central London might not sound like the friendliest place to spend an afternoon. But the staff here are so welcoming that you'll feel at home straight away, even when you find yourself among a herd of sea-blue glass horses (by Ugo Rondinone) or a collection of Sarah Lucas' sensual stuffed-tights sculptures. The gallery's history goes back to the early 90s when its eponymous founder launched many of the biggest YBA artists. Now with three sites across Mayfair and Soho, they balance shows by established stars alongside exciting newcomers. If you've ever felt nervous about going into a commercial gallery, this is a great one to start with.

62 Kingly Street, W1B 5QN
Nearest station: Piccadilly Circus
Other locations: Mayfair
sadiecoles.com

Sarah Lucas, *HONEY PIE*, 2020

53

TJ BOULTING

Independent gallery showcasing original artists

With the beaten-up sofa in the corner and heaving bookcases, you might feel like you've just stepped into someone's living room when first entering the building, but head downstairs and you'll find yourself in a perfectly white-walled gallery space. Past exhibitions have included an art rave, with full-volume techno and ultra-violet paintings by Kate Dunn. Make yourself at home and check out the bathroom – this bonafide art toilet is actually an installation by artist Rachael Haines, who uses gaffer tape to create geometric patterns associated with Tudor architecture. Haines' playful, genre-bending work is a prime example of what this gallery does best – celebrating artists who all possess an irreverent originality.

59 Riding House Street, W1W 7EG
Nearest station: Oxford Circus
tjboulting.com

T.J. BOULTING & SONS
RANGE & STOVE
MANUFACTORY
ESTABLISHED 1808
RIDING HOUSE
STREET W1
T.J. BOULTING & SONS
GAS & ELECTRICAL
ENGINEERS EST. 1808

Boo Saville, *Ma*, 2022

54

THE PHOTOGRAPHERS' GALLERY

Pioneering photography from around the world

Since opening as the UK's first public gallery dedicated to photography in 1971, the Photographers' Gallery has offered a snapshot of the very best lens-based art, whether it's digital photomontage or hand-developed prints shot on vintage hardware. Head downstairs to the bookshop for an unrivalled collection of photography books or, if you fancy starting your own collection, check out the print sales room – it has an expert selection of emerging and established names. Prices aren't cheap but they are certainly more affordable than nearly every other comparable gallery, plus all profits go back to supporting the gallery's programmes. So, let the staff don their white gloves and show you what's available.

16–18 Ramillies Street, W1F 7LW
Neatest station: Oxford Street
thephotographersgallery.org.uk

THE PHOTOGRAPHERS' GALLERY
THE PHOTOGRAPHERS' GALLERY

55

SERPENTINE GALLERY

Contemporary art in Hyde Park

Comprising two separate galleries (one occupying an old teahouse, the other housed in a repurposed gun store), the Serpentine has been championing contemporary art since 1970 but only recently has it garnered a reputation for exhibiting art that explores new technologies and augmented reality. Visit during the summer and not only will the surrounding park be in full bloom (you can even bring your swimsuit and take a dip in the nearby Serpentine lake), but also you'll get to see the gallery's annual temporary pavilion. This artist-designed meeting space is commissioned each year to champion experimental architecture and usually hosts a whole plethora of one-off live events.

Kensington Gardens, W2 3XA
Nearest station: Knightsbridge
serpentinegalleries.org

SERPENTINE GALLERY

56

THE FITZROVIA CHAPEL

Gothic chapel turned gallery space

You could walk past the Fitzrovia Chapel for years without ever knowing it's there. Hidden in a sea of newly developed luxury flats and totally unassuming from the outside, it's now all that remains of the since demolished Middlesex Hospital. Regular art exhibitions often give a nod to the building's medical past (like Lee Miller's photos of WW2 nurses or the costumes of queer icon and former patient Leigh Bowery). Once inside, the gold ceiling, mosaic floor, stained glass windows and gothic arches will delight even the most hardened Londoner – it's an artwork in itself and proves that gallery spaces don't need to be all white walls and no personality.

2 Pearson Square, W1T 3BF
Nearest station: Oxford Circus
fitzroviachapel.org

Lee Miller: Nurses, 2022

57

SKETCH

Iconic restaurant with art-led interiors

Art is infused into every corner of this extraordinary multi-venue eatery. Of course, sketch is most well-known for its insta-perfect restaurant, recently given a rose-gold-tinted makeover by architect India Mahdavi and artist Yinka Shonibare. Dine on hand-dived scallops while taking in the visual playfulness of Shonibare's vivid artworks (which include masks and framed quilts) hanging against metallic walls. Prices are silly and the Swarovski-crystal toilets are even sillier. Can't afford to splurge? Afternoon tea is a (slightly) more affordable option.

9 Conduit Street, W1S 2XG
Nearest station: Oxford Circus
sketch.london

58

THE WALLACE COLLECTION

Magnificently over-the-top opulence

This stately home turned museum is pure maximalism. Think gold-flocked wallpaper, suits of armour engraved with flowers, and countless reclining nudes. Their collection of old masters (make sure you see Fragonard's ridiculously rococo *The Swing*) and decorative arts is pretty much unrivalled in London. Stroll through lavishly ornate Louis XIV furniture and cabinets full of jewelled daggers, before relaxing with a cup of tea in the vast pink-walled courtyard restaurant. Flooded with light from the glass ceiling, it's dotted with antiquities and maple trees – though look closer and you'll see that the trees, at least, are fakes.

Manchester Square, W1U 3BN
Nearest station: Bond Street
wallacecollection.org

59

THE ROYAL ACADEMY

Eminently excellent art institution for all

This prestigious establishment might have a reputation for being stuffy, given its history as a bit of an Enlightenment-era boys' club, but it is really anything but. While the (dependably fantastic) block-buster shows look back over the careers of illustrious artists like Phyllida Barlow and Picasso, there's still plenty of innovation within these hallowed walls, much of which is shown in the always joyous (and joyously unkempt) Summer Exhibition, a sort of wild free-for-all where anyone can apply to show their work alongside illustrious counterparts. And if you really want to see into the future, don't miss the totally charming children's version (the Young Artists' Summer Show). As Picasso said, 'It took me four years to paint like Raphael, but a lifetime to paint like a child.'

Burlington House, Piccadilly, W1J 0BD
Nearest station: Green Park
Paid entry to some exhibitions
royalacademy.org.uk

Burlington House
Royal Academy of Arts
Geological Society
Royal Society of Chemistry
Society of Antiquaries
Royal Astronomical Society
Linnean Society
Burlington House
RA
David Hockney RA
RA
Open late Friday and Saturday
Royal Academy of Arts
RA
Summer Exhibition 2016
Burlington House
Royal Academy of Arts
Geological Society
Royal Society of Chemistry
Society of Antiquaries
Royal Astronomical Society
Linnean Society

Copy of Leonardo da Vinci's *The Last Supper*, c.1515

IMAGE CREDITS

180 The Strand © Jack Hems / courtesy of 180 Studios at 180 The Strand; The Approach (first image) © FXP PHOTOGRAPHY. Courtesy of The Approach, London; The Approach (second image, Kira Freije, *meteorites*, 2022) © Michael Brzezinski. Courtesy of the artist and The Approach, London; The Approach (third image, Sara Cwynar, *Marilyn*, 2020) © Jedrzej Nyka. Courtesy of the artist and The Approach, London; Autograph (intro, p.9), Lina Iris Viktor: *Some Are Born To Endless Night — Dark Matter* at Autograph London. 13 September - 25 January 2020. Curated by Renée Mussai. Photograph © Ben Reeves; Autograph (first image) © Arcaid Images / Alamy Stock Photo; Autograph (second image), Zanele Muholi: *Somnyama Ngonyama, Hail the Dark Lioness* at Autograph, London. 24 July - 28 October 2017. Curated by Renée Mussai. Photograph © Zoë Maxwell; Art Social Club © @ellie.inlondon; Atlantis Art Materials © Martin Usborne; Barbican Art Gallery © Taran Wilkhu; Bold Tendencies (first image, Simon Whybray, *hi boo I love you* © Deniz Guzel, courtesy of Bold Tendencies 2022; Bold Tendencies (second image, Harold Offeh, *Hail the New Prophets* © Damian Griffiths, courtesy of Bold Tendencies 2022; bookart-bookshop © bookartbookshop; Camden Art Centre (installation view of Allison Katz, *Artery*, 2022) © Rob Harris; Candid Arts Trust © Robert Evans / Alamy Stock Photo; Caribbean Fruits (Veronica Ryan, *Custard Apple (Annonaceae), Breadfruit (Moraceae) and Soursop (Annonaceae)*) © Andy Keate; Cass Art Flagship © CASS ART; Chewing Gum Man © PjrNews / Alamy Stock Photo; Chisenhale Gallery (installation view of Rachel Jones, *say cheeeeese*, 2022. Commissioned and produced by Chisenhale Gallery, London) © Andy Keate. Courtesy of the artist; Choosing Keeping © Lesley Lau; Dark Room © Phillip Grey; domobaal (installation view of Lothar Götz, *Salvation*, 2020) © Andy Keate. Courtesy of the artist and domobaal 2020; Dulwich Picture Gallery © Taran Wilkhu; Fitzrovia Chapel (exhibition view of Lee Miller, *Nurses*, 2022) © Tom Carter. Courtesy Fitzrovia Chapel; Fitzrovia Chapel, exhibition view of Lee Miller, *Nurses*, 2022 © Lee Miller Archives, England 2022. All rights reserved. leemiller.co.uk; The Fourth Plinth (intro, p.2) © Amer Ghazzal / Alamy Stock Photos; The Fourth Plinth © Paul Carstairs / Alamy Stock Photo; Frieze Sculpture Park (intro, p.8) © PjrTravel / Alamy Stock Photo; Gagosian © Courtesy Gagosian; Guts Gallery (Sophie Vallance Cantor, *AUTISTIC BITCH*, 2022) © Guts Gallery. Courtesy of the artist; Hayward Gallery (first image), installation view of Lina Iris Viktor, *Eleventh*, 2018. In the Black Fantastic at Hayward Gallery 2022 © the artist; photograph © Rob Harris. Courtesy of Hayward Gallery; Hayward Gallery (second image) © Paul

Carstairs / Alamy Stock Photo; Hauser & Wirth (first image), © Hauser & Wirth London. Courtesy Hauser & Wirth. Photo: Todd White; Hauser & Wirth (second image) © Hauser & Wirth London, 2022. Courtesy Hauser & Wirth; ICA © Photo-Loci / Alamy Stock Photo; Jealous Gallery (Jealous East, Jealous 10th Birthday Celebrations) © Dunja Opalko; Sir John Soane's Museum © Gareth Gardner; Kenwood House (first image) © Taran Wilkhu; Kenwood House (second and third images) © English Heritage; L. Cornelissen & Son © Rachel Smith Photography Ltd; Leake Street Tunnel © Jansos / Alamy Stock Photo; The Line © Angus Mills; M.Y.O © Fiona Caroline Photography; The Lord Napier Star © Frank Da Silva / www.FDAS.co; OOF Gallery (first image) © Tom Carter. Courtesy OOF Gallery; OOF Gallery (second image) © F3 Architects; National Gallery (first image) © Kamira / Alamy Stock Photo; National Gallery (second image) © The National Gallery; Now Gallery (Lydia Chan, *Your Ship Has Landed*, 2021–22) © Charles Emerson; The Painted Hall, Greenwich © Old Royal Naval College; Photographers' Gallery © Luke Hayes; Print Club London © IPJ London, Interiors and Furniture consultants; QUEERCIRCLE (first image) © Taran Wilkhu; QUEERCIRCLE (second image) Deniz Guzel; The Royal Academy (first image) © Steve Vidler / Alamy Stock Photo; Royal Academy Collection Gallery (second image) © James Harris; Royal Drawing School © Angela Moore; Sadie Coles HQ (intro, p.4–5), installation view, Ugo Rondinone, *a sky . a sea . distant mountains . horses . spring .*, Sadie Coles HQ Kingly St, London, 12 April – 14 May 2021 © Ugo Rondinone. Courtesy of the artist and Sadie Coles HQ, London. Photo: Eva Herzog; Sadie Coles HQ, installation view, Sarah Lucas, *HONEY PIE*, Sadie Coles HQ, London, 16 March – 8 August © Sarah Lucas. Courtesy of Sadie Coles HQ, London. Photo: Robert Glowacki; Sarabande Foundation Summer Show 2022 © Sarabande Foundation; Serpentine © David Brabiner / Alamy Stock Photo; Sessions Arts Club (first image) © Louise Long; Sessions Arts Club (second and third images) © Beth Evans; The Showroom (all images) © Dan Weill Photography / Adam Sheild. Courtesy of the artist and The Showroom; sketch (first image) © Edmund Dabney; sketch (second image) © sketch; South London Gallery © Andy Stagg; Studio Voltaire © Mark Blower. Courtesy of Studio Voltaire; Tate Britain (first image) © Michael Jones / Alamy Stock Photo; Tate Britain (second image) © Malcolm Park / Alamy Stock Photo; Tate Modern (first image) © Edmund Sumner-View / Alamy Stock Photo; Tate Modern (second image) © Tony French / Alamy Stock Photo; Tate Modern (third image) © Taran Wilkhu; TJ Boulting (all images) © TJ Boulting; Turning Earth © Turning Earth; Victoria Miro © Photo-Loci / Alamy Stock Photo; The Wallace Collection (intro, p.6–7) © Alison Wright; The Wallace Collection © The Wallace Collection; White Cube: Louise Giovanelli, *Prairie*, 2022, Oil on linen, Overall: 118 1/8 x 212 5/8 in. (300 x 540 cm), Three panels, each: 118 1/8 x 70 7/8 in. (300 x 180 cm), © the artist. Photo © White Cube (Ollie Hammick). Courtesy of the artist and White Cube; Whitechapel Gallery © Guy Montagu-Pollock @ Arcaid. Courtesy of Whitechapel Gallery.

INDEX

An Opinionated Guide to Art London
First edition

Published in 2022 by Hoxton Mini Press, London

Text by Christina Rose Brown
Copy-editing by Octavia Stocker
Design by Richard Mason
Production by Sarah-Louise Deazley
Production and editorial support by Alison Evans

With thanks to Matthew Young for initial series design.

Please note: we recommend checking the websites listed for each entry before you visit for the latest information on price, opening times and pre-booking requirements.

A CIP catalogue record for this book is available from the British Library.

ISBN: 978-1-914314-30-8

Printed and bound by OZGraf, Poland

Hoxton Mini Press is an environmentally conscious publisher, committed to offsetting our carbon footprint. This book is 100 percent carbon compensated, with offset purchased from Stand For Trees.

For every book you buy from our website, we plant a tree:
www.hoxtonminipress.com